Dinosaur Facts for Kids

Animal Book for Kids
Children's Animal Books

BABY PROFESSOR

EDUCATION KIDS

Speedy Publishing LLC
40 E. Main St. #1156
Newark, DE 19711
www.speedypublishing.com

Copyright 2017

All Rights reserved. No part of this book may be reproduced or used in any way or form or by any means whether electronic or mechanical, this means that you cannot record or photocopy any material ideas or tips that are provided in this book

In this book, we're going to cover the fascinating world of prehistoric dinosaurs. So, let's get right to it!

Life has existed on planet Earth for about four billion years. For most of that time, the organisms that lived on Earth were of the simplest form. Most were microorganisms that began life in the waters of the oceans.

EXTINCTION BEFORE AND EXTINCTION AFTER

Then, about 542 million years ago, everything started to transform. More sophisticated animals and plants began to appear. They spread everywhere on both the lands and the seas.

Permian-Triassic boundary

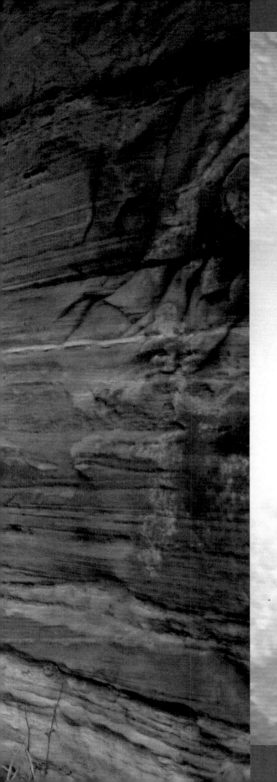

At the end of the Paleozoic Era, there was a mass extinction and most of the animals and plants died out. This event, now called the Permian-Triassic extinction, occurred about 245 million years ago and it took over 30 million years for life on Earth to recover.

The animals that survived this mass extinction eventually evolved into the dinosaurs. This era, when dinosaurs roamed the Earth as their domain, lasted for about 185 million years from 250 million years ago to 65 million years ago. Then, a second mass extinction event led to the end of these amazing creatures. This event marked the end of the Mesozoic Period and the beginning of the Cenozoic Period, which continues through today.

WHAT WERE THE DINOSAURS?

Dinosaurs evolved from the archosaurs, a group of egg-laying reptiles that managed to survive the devastating Permian-Triassic Extinction. Two other groups of reptiles were descended from the archosaurs, too.

Tyrannosaurus rex

They were the pterosaurs, which were flying creatures, and crocodiles. The dinosaurs were different from these two groups. Dinosaurs were land creatures and they walked in one of two ways. Some walked upright on two legs like our modern birds and had smaller front appendages.

Tyrannosaurus Rex

Tyrannosaurus rex was a good example of this posture. If they had four equally sized legs, they walked with their legs stiff and straight. This straight-legged posture was unlike how the crocodiles move since their legs spread out under them when they walk.

HOW DO WE KNOW ABOUT DINOSAURS?

Even though dinosaurs haven't lived on Earth for 65 million years, scientists know a lot about them. The reason is that the Earth itself holds clues about the lives of dinosaurs in the fossil record.

Paleontologists, scientists who study fossils, have been able to piece together skeletons of dinosaurs. Dinosaur fossils were found as early as 1676, but it wasn't until 1841 when a British scientist by the name of Richard Owen realized that these fossils weren't from iguanas or giant people. He recognized that they were different from any living creature and named them "Dinosauria," which translates to "terrible lizards."

Richard Owen

WHAT ARE FOSSILS?

Fossils are the preserved remains of dead animals and plants. When a dinosaur died, it was frequently stuck in mud and couldn't get out. Its body was covered over very quickly by sand or mud and its body was encased.

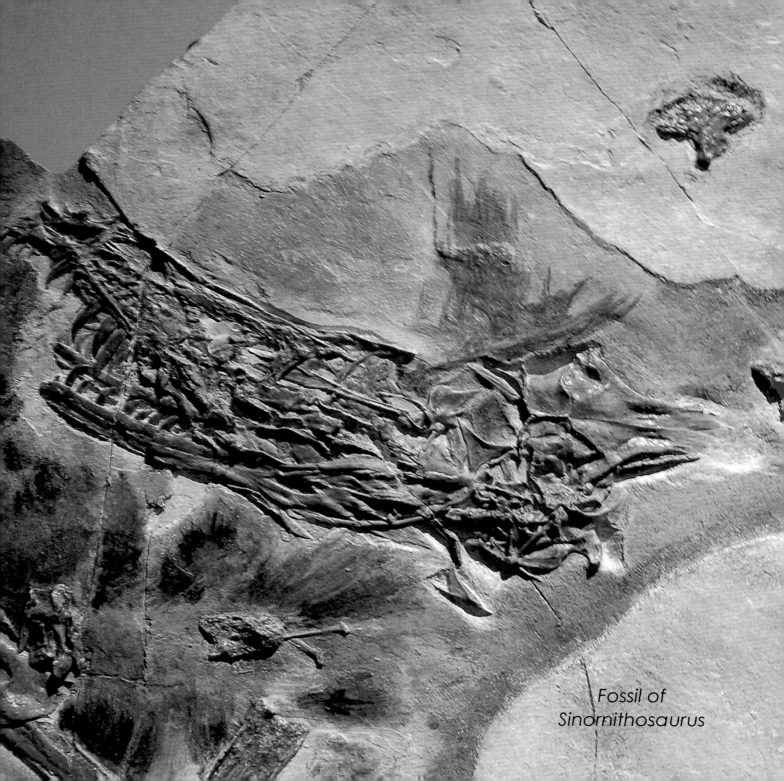

Fossil of
Sinornithosaurus

Psittacosaurus fossil

After a period of time, the sand or mud solidified into rock. Gradually, water seeped through the veins of the rock. It carried away fragments of the bones and replaced them with minerals.

Dinosaur Bones

Over a long period of time, the remaining bones petrified, which simply means that they turned into stone copies of the original parts. At the beginning, these fossils were discovered by accident, but once scientists figured out that they held clues to animals that were no longer on Earth, there was lots of interest in finding out more about them.

Paleontologists sought out areas where they suspected that dinosaur bones could be found. Large bones are much more likely to become fossils than tiny ones, so this may be the reason why so many of the species that paleontologists have categorized today are of the larger varieties of dinosaurs.

Allosaurus eating

WHAT KIND OF FOOD DID THEY EAT?

Dinosaurs had a much more varied diet than what most people think. There were three different types of diets, just as animals have today. Herbivores ate a strict plant diet, omnivores ate plants and some meat, and carnivores ate meat.

Some types of dinosaurs ate eggs, early mammals, lizards and turtles. The more ferocious carnivores hunted and killed other dinosaurs to eat or they were scavengers and ate dead animals. The majority of species ate plants. They didn't eat grass because grass hadn't evolved yet.

Inostrancevia

Brontosaurs

The fossils that contain dinosaur bones also contained many different types of pollen and spores. This has led paleontologists to believe that there were thousands of varieties of plants during the Mesozoic Era for dinosaurs to choose from. They had conifers, like pine trees and redwoods.

They also had ferns and mosses of all types. There's still debate about when flowering plants appeared on Earth, but it's known that before the mass extinction, dinosaurs had added fruit to their diets as well. Many of the herbivores had cheek pouches that allowed them to store their food for quite a while before digesting it.

Dinosaur Replica

WERE THEY ALL BIG?

We generally think that all dinosaurs were enormous beasts that made the earth tremble when they walked. Actually only a few types of dinosaurs were this size. The largest ones were bigger than several houses and were the largest animals that ever lived on our planet.

The smaller ones were as tiny as chickens. They had different body features too. Some had very tough hides like the hides of elephants. Some had lots of scales like lizards and many had neck frills, spikes and horns that helped them with hunting and defending themselves. Paleontologists believe that some had feathers like modern-day birds.

Dinosaurs
Fighting

Based on their diets, some were speedy, aggressive hunters and others slowly ambled and moved from plant to plant to eat. Scientists don't know for sure, but there's evidence that some were more active during the day and others, who were equipped with large eyes for night vision, used the night to hunt and forage.

Some dinosaur egg fossils have been found as well. The smallest egg that was found was the size of a tennis ball and the biggest was the size of a large cannonball!

WHY DID THEY GO EXTINCT?

Almost all scientists agree that dinosaurs eventually went extinct after a huge asteroid hit the Earth. In 2014, a group of researchers got together to look at the other factors that caused this mass extinction.

Victorian Dinosaurs

Triceratops

They studied all the available data they had on the late Cretaceous period, which was the time period in the final one-third of the Mesozoic period right before the extinction occurred. By studying the available fossil records carefully, they discovered that the populations of large plant-eating dinosaurs, such as duck-bills and triceratops, had started to get smaller during that time.

It's not unusual for animals' populations to decrease. Eventually, the populations increase again. However, these decreased populations combined with the devastation of the asteroid event were what caused the mass extinction. The asteroid created a huge crater in the land area that is now Mexico. The crater it left behind is 200 kilometers in width. The blow to the Earth's crust caused terrible tsunamis in the oceans worldwide as well as killer earthquakes.

Diplodocus

There were fires that erupted near the crater and gases and dust spewed into the atmosphere, which blocked the sun for a long time. Without their normal levels of sunlight, plants started to die, which then caused the waning populations of herbivores to die out. Without herbivores to eat, the big carnivores died out too.

Carcharodontosaurus vs Spinosaurus

Eighty percent of life on Earth died out during this time. It was almost as devastating as the Permian-Triassic Extinction had been. Once the dinosaurs had completely died out, the species of mammals that remained began to thrive. If the dinosaurs hadn't died out, mammals would probably not have been able to thrive and evolve into our ancestors. Human beings might not have been a part of Earth's history at all.

BIGGEST AND SMALLEST DINOSAURS

There are always debates about the sizes of dinosaurs and new fossils are being found all the time. The biggest dinosaur we have information about is the Argentinosaurus. It weighed as much as 100 tons and was over 120 feet long. It needed to eat 100,000 calories daily to get to adult size.

Argentinosaurus

The smallest may have been the Microraptor. It might have been mistaken for a very strange pigeon with four wings. It was part of the Velociraptor family, but it only measured around two feet from head to tail.

DINOSAURS EVOLVED INTO BIRDS

Over the last decade, paleontologists have discovered evidence that our modern-day birds evolved from dinosaurs called maniraptoran theropods. These dinosaurs were relatively small meat-eaters and include the Velociraptors made famous by the movie Jurassic Park. So, next time you hear a bird outdoors, think about how they wouldn't be around if it weren't for their ancestors, the dinosaurs.

Visit

BABY PROFESSOR
EDUCATION KIDS

www.BabyProfessorBooks.com

to download Free Baby Professor eBooks
and view our catalog of new and exciting
Children's Books

49720926R00038

Made in the USA
Middletown, DE
21 October 2017